From Despair to Repair:
Lord, Continue to Order Our Steps

Michael Todd
and
Cheryl Ryan-Todd

This book is a work of non-fiction, with ideas and events recalled from both the authors' memory.

CLF Publishing, LLC.
9161 Sierra Ave, Ste. 203C
Fontana, CA 92335
www.clfpublishing.org

Cover Design by Senir Design. Contact information
info@senirdesign.com.

ISBN # 978-1-945102-19-6

Printed in the United States of America.

Dedications

*This book is dedicated first and foremost to God,
who is the Lord of our lives.*

*Furthermore, this book is dedicated to the memory of
Michael's son Jason and grandson Albert, Jr.*

*And, a special dedication goes to Elizabeth Lasky,
Cheryl's mother.*

Acknowledgements

We acknowledge the following individuals for their impact upon our lives, either individually or collectively.

Michael's parents: Morgan City and Gloria Todd.

*Our publisher at CLF Publishing, LLC,
Dr. Cassundra White-Elliott, who was patient with us
as she guided us throughout this journey.*

*And, we acknowledge each other because without
love, understanding, and effective communication,
this book would not have come to fruition.*

Table of Contents

Introduction

Just like any other couple, Michael and Cheryl led separate lives until the day their paths crossed.

Prior to that moment, Michael grew up in a stable household with loving parents, who were concerned about his wellbeing. They taught him morals, responsibility, and the importance of fatherhood, should he one day father children. Sure enough, Michael fathered several children. However, although he was in one relationship after another, he never 'tied the knot' of holy matrimony. Nevertheless, his heart longed for the perfect mate.

Leaving his parents' stable home, Michael found himself in several precarious situations, where he had to make one decision after another. Some decisions proved favorable, while others proved to be life changing. After several bumps along the way, Michael would eventually find himself on a path that would bring glory to God.

Cheryl, unlike Michael, did not have the blessing of growing up in a stable household. Nevertheless, throughout the difficulties she experienced as a youth, she had loving sisters who always cared about her wellbeing, just as she did for theirs. Being left to understand love on her own, due to the absence of a father to raise her, Cheryl found herself looking for love in the arms of men. As time progressed, Cheryl would finally reckon with herself that what appeared to be on the outside of a person was not necessarily what was present on the inside.

Once their paths crossed, Michael and Cheryl forged an unbreakable bond. The Bible says in Ecclesiastes 4:12, a three-strand cord is not easily broken. With the two of them bound together with the Lord Jesus in the midst, their union is solid.

Read the story of their individual and collective journeys and see how the power of God kept them along the way.

His Story

Michael William Todd

Chapter One ~ Life Away From Home

High school was an exciting time in my life. It brought many adventures as well as many challenges. In December 1972, when I was on winter break during my freshman year of high school, I met Teresa, a beautiful seventeen-year-old girl at the Hollywood Skating Rink, on Hollywood and Western, in Los Angeles. After watching her for a while, I invited her to couple skate, which was the last skate to the last song of the night. She said if I would walk her to the bus stop afterward, she would skate with me. I agreed to her request, and she consented to mine. Our skate was the beginning of a three-year relationship that I would have with her from the time I was fourteen to the time I was seventeen.

After winter break, when school resumed in January, Teresa was looking forward to completing her senior year, while I was still getting my sophomore year fully underway. But, things weren't going as smoothly as Teresa would have liked. She informed me she was ten credits short of graduating, and graduation was only six months away- in June. To ensure she graduated in a timely manner, I enrolled her into Jefferson High School's night program, and she attended classes on Tuesday and Thursday night. To guarantee she completed her classwork and homework, I attended classes with her although I was not enrolled. That June, my girlfriend graduated high school. But there was one thing that was different about her than the other girls: She was one month pregnant. The next year in February of 1974, she gave birth to our daughter Michelle Lakeisha Todd.

One month later, the three of us began living together and continued to do so until four months before I graduated high school, which was approximately a year and a half later. Teresa decided the relationship wasn't working for her, and she asked me to leave.

During the year and a half that Teresa and I lived together, my mother would constantly ask my brother Kenneth, who was one year older than I was, if I was at school. Daily, he assured her I was present.

After Teresa and I broke up, I moved back home with my parents and finished the last four months of my senior year and graduated high school in June 1975.

After graduating high school, I incessantly looked for a job but was continuously unsuccessful. I needed to provide for my daughter as well as myself, so I saw no other alternative except to join the United States Marine Corps. At the same time, I was looking forward to serving my country. On December 27, 1975, I left to Concord, California for a three-year stent in the Corps. I started off as a grunt and worked my way up to military police officer.

During my time in the service, I was able to go home each weekend, provide for my daughter, and send $25 savings bonds home to her, which she was later able to use for college. The Marines changed my life. I went from being an immature, young boy to being a mature man. My ideas changed, my dreams were developed, and my life goals were expanded. Furthermore, I learned to develop a five and ten-year plan for my life. After three years of spending time in the Corps and maturing both mentally and physically, in 1978, I changed from active duty to reserves, which I engaged in for three years, from 1978 to 1981.

During that same time frame, not only did I love serving my country, but I also had a love for dancing. In September 1975, a new friend of mine connected me with the television show *Soul Train*. For one month, as part of a dance team, I danced on *Soul Train*. That was an exciting time for me, and I was able to meet some of the great African-American singers, such as Al Green, Patti LaBelle, the Spinners, Minnie Rippleton, etc. The friend that connected me with *Soul Train* was Deborah Marie Jones. During our interaction, we began a relationship, and from our union, we conceived a son who we named Michael Todd, Jr. He was born in 1977. Our relationship lasted for six years after coming to an end for one of the strangest reasons known to man: Deborah wanted to have a relationship with my brother Morgan, and he felt the same way. Unbeknownst to me, Morgan and Deborah had been secretly seeing each other when I would be away from home at work. At that time, I worked graveyard, and no sooner than I would leave my home, Morgan would come over. On some days, he would still be there when I arrived home. But, I thought nothing of it because Deborah would be doing his hair, of which I was aware. After some time though, their involvement was revealed to me by Deborah's sister Donna by way of a telephone call. After being apprised of the situation, I confronted the two of them about their entanglement. At first they denied it. However, as I continued to press the issue, they finally admitted they had been sleeping together. To say the least, I was very hurt and felt betrayed by them both.

At their request, I moved out, and my brother moved in. I went through a period of depression after the break up with Deborah. The bout of depression lasted for five months, and during that time, my father took me to Canada to get my mind off the situation. It is my firm belief that time cures all wounds. I was completely devastated - not so much about the break up between Deborah and myself, but I actually felt as though I had lost my son- to another man- my brother, who had the audacity to tell me not to worry about Mike, Jr because he would take care of him.

One month later, Deborah and Morgan were married and moved to Hawaii, where my brother was being stationed, as he had just joined the Army. They remained in Hawaii for three and a half years. Afterward, Deborah and Morgan returned to the mainland. However, one year and a half later, Morgan went to jail on a drug charge and divorced Deborah while inside.

Meanwhile, once I had returned from my five-month trip, Deborah's sister Donna and I began a relationship, and I moved in with her and her aunt. From our four-year union, we had three children: Jason, Myesha, and Jonathan. Donna and I even attempted to get married in Las Vegas. But because she was under age at seventeen, it was a 'no go.' Her aunt, with whom we lived, told me she had guardianship over at Donna, and she consented to the marriage. However, when we went to the court, we found out her aunt did not actually have legal guardianship over Donna. Her father, who was still living, did. Therefore, the court denied our request. At the end of our four-year relationship, I left Donna and moved back home with my parents. Donna eventually left California, taking my three children with her, and moved back to New Orleans.

Sometime later, while living at my parents' home, I woke up one morning, looked outside, and saw Deborah sleeping in my father's truck, which was parked in the front yard. I woke up Morgan and told him Deborah was outside, and his only response was, "I'm done with her." Unfortunately, Deborah was strung out on drugs, and she had come to our home looking for some, while leaving our ten-year-old son alone at home. I promptly called a cab, placed Deborah in it, and sent her back home. About a week later, I put my son on a plane and sent him to Deborah's father, knowing that would be a safer environment for him. About a week after that, Deborah herself went back to New Orleans. To this day, neither of them has returned to California.

As time went on, I met a woman named Sandra, and she and I conceived a son together. However, at the time, she did not tell me he was my son. She always claimed he was the son of a drug dealer with whom she was involved. However, when my son was fourteen years old and the man who was supposedly his father had died, I saw them in a grocery store, and Sandra lifted her hand, pointed at me, and told my son, "Hey, there is your daddy." Since that time, I have attempted to foster a healthy relationship with my son, just as I have with all my children.

A Point to Ponder

As a young man, I engaged in one relationship after another from the time I passed through puberty. I was a young man in school, trying to earn an education. Although I graduated high school at the scheduled time and had done well with my studies, what did I have to offer a young woman when I was still relying upon my parents to provide guidance and a roof over my head?

~~~~~~~~~~

To all the young people who may be reading this book- Before you enter into a relationship with another person, trying to offer him/her a better life, make sure your life is together. When two people are complete as individuals and have a solid foundation, they will make a strong unit. Otherwise, it is easy for chaos and uncertainty to enter and cause further confusion.

I learned- once I was older- time is the best teacher because with experience comes lessons learned. Those lessons make you better prepared for life. As a youth, one should explore and learn him/herself before engaging in a life-changing relationship with someone else.

Chapter Two ~ Family Matters

Life is full of its ups and downs. Life begins and life ends. The Bible says in Hebrews 9:27, *"It is appointed unto Men once to die."* We must all travel that way. In a period of ten years, I lost seven people who are very dear to my heart, and their deaths impacted me greatly. All of them will forever have a special place in my heart.

My Dear Love

In 1986, my beloved mother Gloria Ruth Todd, one day seemingly out of nowhere, began to suffer from shortness of breath and pains in her chest. Immediately, she was taken to the hospital and when she arrived, she was admitted for tests. Her stay at the hospital lasted for a couple of days, and during that time a heart murmur was detected. All of her children, including myself, were very fearful of what the diagnosis meant for her. We were all greatly concerned because prior to that incident, she had had no other hospital visits, emergencies, or urgent concerns.

Her doctor recommended a change in diet because she had high blood pressure and high cholesterol. My siblings and I set to work scheduling a caregiver for her, to ensure someone would be with her around-the-clock. Because I worked the swing shift from 7 PM to 2 AM, my siblings and I decided it would be best if I served as her caregiver during the day hours. So for three years, I took care of her on a daily basis. I changed her diet to a no-grease and no-fried food diet. I only fed her broiled and baked meats. I also changed from salt to using Mrs. Dash. Over a three-year time frame, she lost seventy pounds and was in much better health.

However, at the end of February in 1989, on a Monday evening, my mother passed in her sleep when she stopped breathing. CPR was administered, and the ambulance came. Immediately, they placed her on a breathing machine. However, when she arrived at Daniel Freeman Hospital, the doctor explained to us that there was a period when no oxygen had gone to her brain. She was placed on life-support, and we were told we had to make a decision within a week: to keep her on life-support or to remove her. That decision was taken out of our hands when the Lord took her four days later, on that Thursday night.

At that point, it was time to prepare for her burial. From that day to the day of the funeral, I could hear my mother's voice telling me exactly what to do regarding the funeral services and my siblings. My youngest brother was very uncooperative during the entire process, and he refused to put on a tuxedo for the funeral, so I ended up replacing him as a pallbearer with my stepbrother Melvin.

On March 5, 1989, we placed my mother to rest. Up to that point, I had not shed a tear, as I was focused on the preparation of her burial. But during the service, I asked for a box of Kleenex, and I wept for the very first time.

Grandma

Approximately one year after the passing of my mother, my maternal grandmother Mary Walton, who was born in 1913, began to experience dementia. My brother Raymond and I decided it would be best if we moved in with her and serve as her caregivers. For a year and a half, we fed, bathed, and dressed her. However, as time went on, her brother Leroy decided it would be best to put her in a home. We did not agree with his decision, but because he was the senior member of the family, we respected his voice and his wishes.

So, for the next year and a half of her life, she lived in a convalescent home. One day, in 1992, she requested her family come to see her, and she specifically asked for my brother Mitchell. However, he refused to go. He thought it would be okay to send her some money, thinking that would appease her. In disagreement, I told him, "No, your presence is being requested. You need to go." But no matter how much I pleaded with him, he refused to go.

During our visit with our grandmother, we sang songs and just had a really good time. We ended the visit because she said she was tired, so we decided to leave to allow her an opportunity to rest. And hour after we left, the convalescent home called us and said our grandmother had stopped breathing and had gone into a coma. She stayed in the coma for two days before passing away. My brother Mitchell took it very hard. I assumed he was experiencing a bout of guilt for not having heeded our grandmother's last request of him.

Unc

Near the end of 2001, my uncle Leroy, who was actually my mother's uncle, my grandmother's brother, suffered a stroke, which caused paralysis in the left side of his body. Prior to the stroke, he had been healthy as a horse and as fit as a fiddle. Two months after his stroke, he called me to serve as his caregiver. And I did so for eleven months until his death. Because I worked at night, I could only watch over my uncle during the daytime, so there was a young woman who cared for him in the evenings while I was away. Unfortunately, she did not do as well as I would have liked, but her presence kept him from being alone.

Uncle Leroy was a fun-loving character, and he also was a creature of habit. Every day, he desired the same breakfast, which consisted of over-easy eggs, grits, and two slices of bacon or hotlinks. On Sundays, he liked to go to church, which I helped him to get dressed for. Afterward, he would eat Church's chicken, with coleslaw and corn. As time progressed, I recall being required to pick him up and move him from one place to another because it had become increasingly difficult for him to walk on his own. That particular time of my uncle's life was very difficult for him as a man. I believe he felt he had lost his dignity although our family never saw it that way. To add to his frustration, he had served at West Angeles Church for 36 years as a deacon, and he was very saddened because no one from the ministry had come to visit him until he was ready to leave the hospital, after he had there for 32 days.

I was happy to be able to serve as a caregiver for my uncle. However, there was a specifically difficult time for me during the course of it all. During the last three months of my uncle's life, I would constantly hear him praying to God to take his spirit. Hearing his prayer was very disturbing for me. I had heard others pray for God to heal them and prolong their life, but I had never heard anyone request for his spirit or his soul to be taken. The other difficult part of being a caregiver for my uncle was it required me to move back to the projects after working so hard to get out of there, having lived there for several years. Being in those surroundings was very depressing for me.

Two months prior to my uncle's death, his health took a turn for the worse. His children, who had not visited him anytime during his illness, finally showed up and demanded he be placed in a home. I refused their request and told them to go away. They had never been there for him during any of the time after his stroke to then, and I did not believe their request should be honored.

Finally, on November 10, 2002, the day my uncle had prayed so long for came, and his request was granted. Suddenly, he went into cardiac arrest, and the paramedics were called to his residence. It was necessary that they use the paddles to administer shock treatment, but after the third unsuccessful attempt, I requested that they stop and try no more. My uncle had left us and a tremendous weight was lifted from my shoulders. I had peace at that moment because I knew he was resting in peace.

Dougie Fresh

My father Morgan City Todd was born in 1918, on March 8, in Manning, Louisiana. He had twenty-one siblings, but only three of them were still alive when he departed this earth. He worked in construction for forty years and married my mother in 1954. Although he suffered six heart attacks and was on nitroglycerin, it wasn't his bad heart that took his life. Fluid had built up on his lungs and the doctor was unable to release it. So, my father breathed his last breath at 87 years of age.

Throughout my lifetime, I spent a lot of time with my father creating an unbreakable bond. We spent a lot of time together doing construction work. I can recall an occasion when my father and I were together and we saw one man in a truck pouring concrete, but there was no one on the receiving end to smooth the concrete out. My father walked over, grabbed a long piece of wood, and began smoothing the concrete. I joined in and assisted him. So, both my father and I helped the one man complete the job because his crew had not shown up to do the work they had been assigned to do.

When my father was no longer able work in construction, he ran pool halls. Although my father was a working man and did all he could to support his wife and children, he always had time to spend with us. During our times with him, he showed my brothers and me how to be men and how to raise our children. Because of my father's dedication to me as his son, there was no need for me to look to athletes or actors to be my role models because my father was my hero. It broke my heart when he departed this earth in February 2006. However, I am left with fond memories that I will always cherish.

Big Mitch

My brother Mitchell Parnell Todd, who was lovingly named after my father's best friend, favorite pastime was to watch football. So, one Saturday afternoon, he engaged in watching the infamous UCLA v USC football game. Early the next morning, his son came across his father's body, which was sprawled over the hallway floor, on his way to the restaurant. His son cried out to his mother saying, "Momma, Daddy is on the floor. He doesn't look good. Something's wrong." My brother had suffered a massive heart attack, and his life was gone on that day December 3, 2006.

Although I was grieved and my heart was broken, I found my way to the house of God that same morning. I felt the need to be with my church family and to be in God's presence where I could find solace.

Little Albert

The youngest person to ever come into my life and leave so quickly was my daughter's son Albert, Jr. He was only three months old, and he died from the whooping cough in early 2007. His death was very disturbing to me for many reasons. The main reason was the fact that I never had an opportunity to see my grandson or hold him in my arms.

My Dear Son Jason

Of all the deaths of family members I experienced, one of the most difficult to endure was the death of my own son Jason Todd. Prior to his passing, there was a warning. As the Bible says in Proverbs 16:18, *"Warning comes before destruction."* There was an occasion where nine shots were directed towards my son, and of the nine shots, he was actually only hit once or twice and obviously the wounds were not fatal. However, a time would come when my son would be shot again. He and a friend of his decided to rob a drug dealer and take all his money and drugs. They were successful in their attempt. And instead of fleeing the scene, they decided to go inside the drug dealer's home looking for more. Inside the home, the drug dealer's girlfriend pulled out her weapon and shot my son five times in his upper torso. That time, the shots he received proved to be fatal. On August 22, 2007, my son departed this earth, at only twenty-four years of age.

A Point to Ponder

Family is precious, and it is important to treasure the relationships we have with our family members: parents, siblings, children, and extended family. We never know what the next day will bring, so we must live today as though it is our last day on earth.

Many people waste time holding grudges instead of loving one another. Don't let a day go by without showing your family members how important they are to you. If you wait until they are gone, it will be too late to love on them then. So, don't wait! Love today!

Chapter Three ~ Death and Life

As stated earlier, I served six years total in the Marine Corps. After being out of the service for approximately four or five years, I tried various methods of earning money to support my children and myself. However, year-by-year, I found it increasingly difficult to earn the amount of money that would satisfy our daily needs. So at the age of 28, I began to sell marijuana and cocaine in an effort to support my family. Yes, I was aware that selling drugs was against the law, but I was willing to take the risk in order to feed my children. So, for the next eight years, I engaged in the activity, but the result of my involvement in drug sales would only prove to be detrimental to my life, which was my worst fear.

In high school, I had already begun smoking marijuana and had continued its use into my adult years. However, two years after selling cocaine, while I was spending time with a young lady, she offered me cocaine in primo form, which means the cocaine was crushed and mixed into a cigarette with the tobacco or into a marijuana joint. When she offered it to me, the cocaine was mixed with marijuana. I already knew the 'high' I received from smoking marijuana, and she explained that the high I would receive from the primo would be magnified. So, I decided to take her up on her offer. The sensation I experienced after smoking the primo was like none I had ever felt before. I continued wanting to experience the high, so I smoked cocaine in this form for about a year and a half to two years.

As time went on, I began to desire an elevated high. The sensation the primo gave me was no longer satisfactory. So, I graduated from the primos to crack cocaine. Because I was already selling the drug, having it in my possession made it easier to utilize, and it was actually cheaper than the primo form because I no longer had to have marijuana in my possession or purchase the zigzags that were required to roll the cigarettes. All I needed was my pipe and the screen that was placed inside which the rock sat on as it melted.

By that time, the drugs had gotten the best of me and had completely changed my life. Unfortunately, I did not know how bad my situation was. But soon, the ugly truth would slowly rear its head and divulge what had been hidden from me. My enlightenment began when on one occasion, I looked sideways in a mirror, and I caught my reflection. By no means did I like what I saw. I had lost sixty pounds without really realizing it, and the weight loss made me very thin. From that point on, rather than addressing my drug habit and attending to my physical needs, I simply refused to view my own reflection. That is one example to demonstrate how the enemy had my mind twisted. He told me there was no way out. I believed him, and it showed in my actions. For example, I would sit in an abandoned truck and smoke my life away.

In this book, I chose to share my experiences publicly, but the reality is reminiscing about my drug abuse is still so very depressing. Normally, when the memories come up in my mind about what I was doing to myself, I put a lid on them and refuse to allow myself to think about it. And during the timeframe when I was using drugs, I did not want my family to know about it or to see me in my broken condition. To my disappointment and I'm sure to theirs, they knew anyway. To try to help me when I would leave home, they would find me, strong arm me, and take me back home. I was so delusional that I couldn't see the complete impact the drugs had on my life. I did not want their help, nor did I believe I needed it.

To further demonstrate my state of delusion, allow me to share another episode. On one occasion, I went to see my father. While standing in front of him, I opened my dirty hand, which was filled with cocaine rocks, and said, "Dad, I'm winning today." I was referring to the amount of rocks I had in my possession that I could later use to get high. His response was simply, "Well, Mike-Mike. I hear what you are saying. But, from the looks of things, it looks as though you are losing." At the time, his comment did not mean much to me. It would be years before I fully comprehended what his words meant and to understand how much seeing me in that condition must have broken his heart. But, through it all, he loved me. For that, I am grateful.

During that devastating time in my life, the enemy stole so much from me: time with my children that I could have used to teach them things and time I could have used to serve God. But, I realize I cannot turn back the hands of time. All I can do is continue to march forward. It was definitely a life lesson, which included levels of torment I unwillingly experienced. There was one level that eventually led me away from crack, as it was so unbearable that I could not and would not continue with my drug use. At that level, I would see demons speed by me. As the Word warns, one demon goes to get seven more to occupy a person's temple. One demon is enough to torment anyone. Imagine the havoc seven demons can rain down in a person's life. One day, I was in a hotel room, with my drugs, but I could not enjoy them. The demons were tearing me up. It was so bad that I left the room in a panic and called my brother. I did not have the nerve or the desire to go back in there. I just could not endure the torture any longer. After that time, I soon learned the road to recovery was surprisingly easy, but I was blinded from it for so long. Although recovery itself was not difficult, after every day use, it took a while for sobriety to come into my life.

A Point to Ponder

Serving my country was one of the best decisions I could have ever made because of the difference it made in my personal life. At the end of my service with the U.S. Marines, I had a strong conviction about what it is to be a man. I truly would not be the same man I had grown to become if it had not been for the teachings and trainings I experienced from military personnel.

Every person needs a mentor, either by way of an individual or by way of an organization, such as the Marine Corps. When choosing a mentor, choose someone who is dedicated, loving, has integrity, has a strong character, is morally sound, and makes wise choices. Furthermore, the person or entity must have your best interest at heart.

~~~~~~~~~~~~

Once you have grown and developed, you too can be a mentor for someone else. If you have the characteristics listed above, you will make a good candidate for a mentor, and you can guide someone into becoming a productive member of society.

Chapter Four ~ Bad Choices and Decisions

In late summer of 1989, I was arrested for drunken and disorderly conduct, while in the city of Cudahy. As a result, I was sentenced to ninety days in jail. Let me explain how jail sentences work. Whatever sentence the judge issues, the person is required to actually serve half the time given. So, for a 90-day sentence, I was required to actually serve 45 days. After completing 39 or 40 days, mentally I was preparing to go home, but the reality was, I was told by one of the guards that I was required to appear in court. I attempted to refute the information by saying I had already gone to court on the charge, but my disagreement was to no avail. To court, I went.

In court, the judge recognized me and said, "Hello, Mr. Todd. Are you Raymond, Kenneth, or Michael?"

To his query, I responded, "I'm Michael." The reason the judge asked me to clarify my first name was because I had been arrested on other occasions, and instead of giving my own name, I would often give one of my brothers' names. I had even given one of my brothers' names when he was serving our country. The judge was not happy about my defamation of my brother's name or character.

In court that day, it was time for the judge to clear up and distribute the charges to the person they actually belonged to. And in that case, it was I.

"Okay," the judge responded. "The district attorney wants you to serve five to seven years for prior charges. However, I'm looking over your record, and you only have a few drug charges. (There was a combination of possession, sells, and under the influence charges.) So, I'm going to offer you this deal one and one time only – a two-year sentence." Before he could finish saying the words "two years," I said, "I'll take it!"

Subsequently, my sentence was to be completed at Chuckwalla State Prison, located in Blythe, California, on D Block, which was minimum security for levels one and two. During the time I spent in jail, I had an opportunity to have a clear mind, unclouded from drugs, to make clear choices. While in the penitentiary, not only was I able to have clear thought processes, but I was able to learn essential skills by working on a construction crew, building curbs around the penitentiary. Also, to acquire additional skills, I went to a plumbing class and learned about PVC, galvanized pipes, etc.

When I wasn't working, I wrote letters for some of the inmates because many were illiterate. I also read their letters when they came in. That experience demonstrated to me just how much God had really blessed me in my life. He had given me the opportunity to have a formal education, and I had taken advantage of it while others had pilfered theirs away. Thankfully, my learning did not occur only outside the prison walls, but inside as well. In addition to learning skills of a trade, in all that I did and saw, one valuable lesson I learned while inside was to get respect, one had to give it.

No matter how much I learned and enjoyed the experience of sobriety from drugs, all the time I was inside, I had one great desire: to get out. But, I learned quickly that getting out was something inmates were not to speak of. That type of discussion could literally incite rage in other inmates, and it could lead to someone getting hurt from jealousy. Furthermore, I quickly learned telephones were another item to stay away from. At one point, there was a riot between Blacks and Hispanics- all because someone had taken someone else's phone time. So, I refrained from using the phones (to keep down confrontation) and wrote letters instead.

Through writing letters, I received my biggest source of encouragement from my daughter Michelle, who wrote me five-page letters each week, and I reciprocated in kind. Furthermore, the Spirit of the Lord kept me encouraged because I had begun reading the Word of God.

Then, one day out of nowhere, someone gave me a piece of mail at approximately four o'clock in the evening. The letter stated to report to R &R for release. To say I was overjoyed and utterly surprised would be a grave understatement.

Upon release, I was given $100 just prior to departing the gate. I was informed that I was required to report to my parole officer, whom I went directly to see before going anywhere else. Upon my arrival, she gave me another $100. The $200 total that I received was standard gate money for inmates when they left their temporary housing at a correctional facility.

Although serving time is not something I would wish on anyone, I thank God because He allowed me to go to prison instead of dying in my sickness of drug abuse. Due to His omnipotence, omnipresence and omniscience, He knew what I would go through and the final outcome. Conversely, I was not privy to such information. Regardless of my lacking prior knowledge to the road I would take at that point in my life, I most certainly thank Him for being my saving grace.

A Point to Ponder

Oftentimes, we take for granted the everyday liberties and forfeit them by breaking rules that have been set to keep order in our modern day society. I was one of those people who wanted to do my own thing and go my own way. For the choices I made, I had to pay the penalty. After doing so, I decided I loved and cherished my freedom much more than I had known. Therefore, the choices I made following my incarceration and subsequent release would ensure my continued stay on the *outside* of the prison walls.

~~~~~~~~~~~~

When making decisions, weigh all the pros and cons. Refrain from being hasty. One wrong choice can set you back for years. Each day should be spent moving forward, not going backward.

Chapter Five ~ Road Back to Christ

In 1978, I really thought I had my life in order. But soon, I would learn that the reality was contrary to my own belief. Quite unexpectedly, a very close friend of mine, whom I had not spoken to in sometime, called me because he and a group of men were planning to record a CD, but they had an open spot that needed to be filled. They needed someone to sing tenor and he heard that I could hold a tune. So, he called me and asked me to sing a few bars for him. I did, and he offered me the position. I humbly accepted the invitation and was very excited to be part of a group that would record a CD. Before the conversation ended, he informed me that practice would take place at a church in approximately three weeks and asked if I was okay with that. I told him it was no problem at all.

Before the next Sunday rolled around, I shared the information with my older brother Big Mitch. I told him I wanted to go by the church and check it out. So, that following Sunday, my brother and I went to the worship service, and lo and behold who did I see? Pastor Wayne Pittman. He and his wife were good friends of mine. I used to play baseball and basketball with Wayne when I was twelve or thirteen years old. He was approximately seven years my senior, and it had been thirty years since we had seen each other. What a reunion it was.

My brother was so taken with the worship and praise that took place in the service that he joined the church that very day. I told him I wanted to return to the church the next week and I would join then. On that Sunday, my brother decided not to go, so I went alone and joined church, just as I had stated. If I can use this analogy, I felt like the woman at the well, who after speaking with Jesus for some time, ran and told everyone about the man she had met who told her everything about herself.

When I returned home that day, I told the woman I was living with and had been dating for quite some time about the new church I had found. The next week, she and her children went to church with me and continued going for several years. It was actually our plan to solidify our relationship through marriage. However, that could not happen until she filed for divorce from the husband from which she had been separated for many years.

Eventually, I moved out of the home, so we could live a godly life without cohabitating. I thought if we both focused on our respective relationship with the Lord, we would eventually join together in holy matrimony. Well, my wishes and desires did not come to pass because she mended her relationship with her husband. I was not happy with her decision, but I certainly understood. I came to understand that my plan was not God's plan. He most certainly knew what was best. After that, I remained single for a two-year period as I fortified my relationship with God, the Father; God, the Son; and God, the Holy Spirit.

And, what makes this entire episode more interesting is we never recorded the CD. That was another instance of God at work - to get me back where I needed to be- with Him.

A Point to Ponder

It has been said God works in mysterious ways. That simply means we do not always understand how God works and why things happen the way they do. Nevertheless, God has a plan for each and every one of our lives. When I went to the church that Sunday with one objective: to join the group, God had another plan.

See, I had a foundation in church, but somewhere along the way, I had lost my way. God was simply reclaiming a soldier in His army and getting me prepared to get on the battlefield.

God has need of me, and He has need of you. When you feel Him tugging at you, answer. You will be amazed at the changes He can make in your life.

Her Story

Cheryl Ryan-Todd

Chapter One ~ Childhood Memories

On August 7, 1959, in the small town of Marysville, California, which is situated in the flatlands of an agricultural area, fifty miles north of Sacramento and thirty miles north of Grass Valley, with only a population of 10,000, I came into this beautiful world. I am the second of four daughters born to my mother. My sister Cynthia Marie, the oldest of the crew, was born two years before I was. A year after my arrival, my sister Catherine Diane made her appearance. Finally, our baby sister Angela Marie was born three years after Catherine. And although it may be a rarity for most sisters, I am fortunate to be very close to *all* my sisters.

My childhood and adolescent years were interesting and fun-filled, while at the same time being confusing and tumultuous. One of the things that made my childhood interesting and comparatively different from others was I had a careless and curious habit of always wanting to escape my environment. For example, when I was four years old, I was at the laundromat with my mother and one of her friends. They were heavily engaged in their conversation and paid me very little attention. Bored with the atmosphere and lack of attention, I decided I no longer wanted to grace the laundromat with my presence. So while my mother was otherwise distracted, I walked out the front door and began traversing the sidewalk.

A police officer, who was familiar with me and my antics, drove by, saw me, picked me up, put me in his car, and asked me where I was coming from and where I was going. I responded to his questions by saying I was at the laundromat with my mother, but I had left because she was drinking beer with a friend of hers, and I was headed elsewhere. The truth was she was drinking 'root beer,' but I had neglected the 'root' in front of the 'beer.' I was four years old and was probably unaware of the difference between the two. But due to my inaccurate description, when the police officer arrived at the laundromat, he gave my mother a serious tongue-lashing.

That episode was just one of the many occasions where I felt the need to escape. Escaping gave me a sense of hyper excitement, as I did not enjoy being confined to one locale at any given time. I had a free spirit, and I wanted my physical being to experience the same independence.

As my life continued, curveballs were thrown at me from one occasion to another, making my life feel like a rollercoaster ride. One occurrence was when I was five years old. What was intended to be a pleasant activity with my siblings turned out to be a very horrific and life-altering experience. At a park, one block from our home, we were swinging, climbing trees, and playing hide-and-seek, as we had done any other day at the park. We were having a wonderfully splendid time, as children should. But our joyous time would come to an end. On that particular day, Virgil, one of the park workers, was going around asking various children if they wanted to see something exciting in the pump house. The pump house was where the sprinkler and electrical system were housed. We had never been inside before, our curiosity led some of the children to tell Virgil yes, while others told him no- either from disinterest or fear of the unknown.

Finally, he decided to approach members of my family. First, he asked my sister Cathy if she wanted to see what was inside. She responded affirmatively, but once inside, she was very disturbed by what he attempted to do to her, and she ran out saying, "No, no, no." When he approached me, I completely ignored my sister's reaction and neglected to see it as a warning. I graciously accepted Virgil's invitation. My 'beware of stranger danger' antennas were not operating effectively on that day. Slowly, I walked down the stairs into the pump house. Virgil requested I position myself against the wall once I was inside. I did as I was told. What he did next was unwelcomed and unexpected. He pulled my pants down and inserted two fingers into my vagina, causing me pain and horror. Right at that moment, Cathy came in and saw what was happening. Immediately, she ran to tell our oldest sister Cynthia and our mother.

Virgil grew frightened, and he attempted to flee the scene. However, his escape would prove futile. With her quick wit, Cynthia wrote down his license plate, and the authorities were summoned. Virgil was apprehended and was sentenced to eight years in jail for the crime he committed against me and as well as crimes he had committed against other children. While the outcome with Virgil was to be celebrated, there was another outcome involving the incident that only caused me more drama and feelings of anxiety. While I was in the pump house with Virgil, some of the neighborhood boys had also come in and saw what he was doing to me, and rather than feeling sympathy for me, they teased me about it incessantly. The teasing created feelings of sadness and remorse. I even felt alienated from the rest of my peers. To make matters worse, over time, the teasing increased, and my stepfather went to speak to the boys' parents, in an attempt to get the teasing to cease.

After the horrible incident with Virgil, my life eventually returned to "normal," and there was no more mention of it. At six and seven years of age, I loved to compose plays and coordinate singing contests in my neighborhood. I would design props and costumes and solicit neighbors' participation for the plays and singing contest. But of course, I was always the star of the show. That was a must. However, when I wasn't busy playing the lead role or trying to out sing my neighbors, my sister Catherine and I would sit on an inner tube and float down Feather River. Oh, what fun that was for us!

However, life was not always so peachy keen. At the age of nine years old, I suffered severe head trauma. A group of people was playing a game, and I thought it would be fun to join in. Despite my efforts to join the game, I was told to move out of their way. Being my usual stubborn and ornery self, I refused to abide by their request and found myself being hit in the head with a golf club. I felt my body vibrate in the vey spot I stood. A weird sensation ran through my body, and I found myself laughing uncontrollably. Strangely, I viewed the situation as hilarious- until I saw the blood running down the side of my face. Instantaneously, I realized the situation was serious. I had thought I could assert my will to be included in the game; however, I quickly learned I would not always be included in what others engaged in, and it was best to heed warnings when they came.

Another wonderful pastime I engaged in, from nine years old until I graduated high school, was playing sports. I loved to have play tetherball, baseball, basketball (even though I wasn't very good at it), and volleyball. My teachers encouraged me to participate in sports, believing the activities would help me to overcome my low self-esteem. They were absolutely correct. The sports allowed me to demonstrate my accomplishments and help me feel competent versus incompetent and incapable.

My low self-esteem may have been a result of my mother's abandonment of my sisters and me when I was twelve years old. (My father had made his exit long before, when I was three). After my mother chose to leave our home, my sisters and I were left to raise ourselves for the next six years. The feeling of abandonment left me feeling unwanted and insecure. Although she did not stay in the home with us any longer, she continued to be responsible for the household bills, and she brought us food on a weekly basis. Periodically, she would come and spend the night with us. I suppose she figured if she provided food, clothing, and shelter, her motherly responsibilities were covered. In addition to the physical needs we had, we needed love and guidance. Fortunately, our grandparents, who lived thirty miles away in Grass Valley, provided the guidance we needed. They played a pivotal role in our lives by teaching us manners and respect. Daily doses of love from a constant adult figure in our lives, however, was lacking. In later days, that void would begin to speak out and require fulfillment.

In addition to my mother leaving when I was twelve, my life took another turn. I began experimenting with oral sex. I believe that change in my behavior was due to not having a father figure to guide me and a mother who was intermittent in my life. A year later at thirteen years of age, physically I was very developed, and my sexual activities increased. I had my first sexual encounter with a boy who I had a major crush on. The experience only lasted five minutes- if that. I was greatly disappointed because I did not feel a thing, and I was left wondering, *This is the big step everyone is talking about?* The experience was very hum drum, and to make matters worse, the boy cared nothing for me while I thought he was the cat's meow.

To compound my state of engaging in underage sexual activity, I was also entangled with a group of teenagers of all races. One of our frequent activities was smoking marijuana while hiding from the cops who drove around our neighborhood. Although we smoked and could be easily considered a 'bad bunch,' we never got into any trouble or broke any laws- well, except for smoking marijuana- that is. The only thing I did was steal a Christmas light from someone's home. And unfortunately, I did get caught. Other than that, we pulled no mean stunts and played no tricks on anyone.

At age thirteen, when I was in junior high school, the plot of my life really began to thicken. I lent my marijuana pipe to one of my friends, and she got caught with it in her possession. While being interrogated by the authorities, she snitched on me, and the police promptly came to the school and arrested me. I was required to spend three days in juvenile hall. To exacerbate the influence of authorities in my life, my mother was called to the scene. She was required to retrieve me after my three-day stay. At that time, possession of marijuana was a felony, and the authorities wanted me to understand the seriousness of my offense.

While I was in juvenile hall, I shared a cell with a girl who was both psychologically and emotionally disturbed. She habitually cut her wrists with glass, which for her was a method of relieving the pain she felt. When the blood ran down her arm, it was as though the pain she felt inside was being released. But, in time, she always felt the need to release it again. I truly felt very sorrow for her. At the time, I felt sorrow for myself as well. Being in juvenile hall was a very scary and lonely experience. However, experiencing the three-day mini vacation did not cause me to discontinue smoking. Nor did it discourage me from using acid, which was another habit I had picked up along the way. Quite frankly, I enjoyed the acid trips, for they gave me an awesome feeling.

As you read the account of this portion of my life, it may sound as though I was on a downward spiral. Thankfully though, my time during my high school years wasn't all filled with drug abuse, hiding from the cops, being engaged in sexual escapades, or dealing with juvenile authorities. I did engage myself constructively, such as being involved in agricultural work. During that season of my life, I acquired a job picking rotten tomatoes in the fields and bins of walnuts, making five dollars for each bin. I was also an almond harvester, a peach picker, and a duck feather puller, for $.25 a duck.

Furthermore, in high school, there was a restaurant on my high school campus called The Lemon Tree. The restaurant was open to students, staff, and faculty. I was enrolled in a course similar to the modern home economics course and was able to work in the restaurant and learn a few skills. That particular job was a nonpaying job, as it offered credits for my high school diploma. So, continuing with my delinquent ways and striving to earn money, each day of high school from tenth grade to twelfth grade, I hid bags of marijuana in my socks and sold them to my peers. At the same time, I smoked marijuana myself, but I continued to go to school every day and earn A's and B's.

My attempts to earn money did not stop there. I did acquire a legal paying job during that same time frame and worked in the Marysville library during my junior and senior year of high school. I certainly had a good time there reading books to the young children and just being in that overall environment. My baby sister and her friends would come to the library to visit me as well, making my days even more enjoyable.

After working in the library during the daytime, our evenings at home were filled with even more excitement. Our house was known as the party house, as everyone knew there were no parents there. Our friends and their friends would come over with bottles of alcohol, and we would smoke and drink the nights away.

Throughout my teenage years, as I developed mentally, physically, and emotionally, to my discovery, I learned I had a bad temper. My bad temper was mirrored in my older sister, and together we had knock down – drag out fights with one another. We would hit each other's heads against the floor, knock holes in the walls, and kick the bathroom door down as we fought. Through it all, we loved one another; we just had an unexplainable aggression that erupted from time to time. Much of the anger and physical violence on my part was due to being a heavy drinker during that time. And because there were no adults in the house- no one to mediate our arguments and altercations- we would fight until tiredness overcame us and caused us to cease physically abusing one another.

Through all of the dysfunction, absence of my mother and a solid father-figure, guidance from my teachers and counselors, working legal and illegal jobs, dealing with an overactive libido, and engaging in physical violence, I did successfully graduate high school at the age of seventeen. And for that, I am proud!

A Point to Ponder

Just because a person grows up in an environment that lacks nurture and guidance does not mean the person cannot love herself enough to grow into a mentally and emotionally strong individual.

However, when the odds are stacked against her, she will have to use every positive avenue available to her to become the person God already predestined her to become.

Chapter Two ~ Job Corps and US Army Girl

In 1977, upon graduating high school, my older sister Cynthia and I joined a government program called Job corps. We reported to 9th street and Figueroa and got settled in. The trip we made by bus from Marysville to Los Angeles so astonished my mind, as I had never seen such a big city. I was flabbergasted.

As part of the job core program, I went to Trade Tech College, taking professional cooking and accounting courses. The job corps participants engaged in many interesting activities, including whale watching, gluing flowers on the floats that would be used in the Rose Bowl Parade, etc.

During my stay in the Job Corp, I met a very intelligent man named Guy, and we developed a boyfriend/girlfriend relationship. Unfortunately, he became very physically and verbally abusive, which caused me to leave the job Corp a year early. Due to the violent nature of the relationship, I needed to leave to protect myself. One example of his unsavory verbally abusive behavior was when we were living together, he would always compliment another woman, causing me to feel inferior.

After breaking off the relationship and moving away, I went back to Marysville. My mother was not happy about my return, and she immediately informed me that I could not stay with her. So, I found myself signing up for the United States Army. However, due to an acne problem that I suffered, I was sent to a doctor in San Francisco to determine if my acne was too severe for entrance into the army. Thankfully, my condition was labeled moderate to severe, and I was granted entrance.

On February 14, 1979, I entered Boot Camp in Columbia, South Carolina at Fort Jackson. My stay was a total of eight weeks. Once I was in the army I had a hard time keeping up physically due to a heart murmur and ask him that. When I was initially tested for any heart conditions or any other abnormalities, the machine was not working properly and I was passed through. This unfortunate occurrence impacted me greatly in the military. For example, I could not run the required eight or nine miles that the soldiers had to run on a daily basis in their combat boots. I also remember on one specific occasion having to run twenty-five miles while wearing seventy pounds of equipment, which included my shovel, my poncho, and my sleeping gear, just to name a few.

In the chow hall, there is no time to talk. We had to eat quickly and move on; then, run to our barracks. Furthermore, I wasn't a good shot. I almost was a 'recycle,' which means I would need to cycle through and re-train. On one occasion, my drill sergeant came into my fox hole and knocked on my helmet and said, "Ryan, you'd better start hitting the target, or you will be a recycle!" At that point, I start hitting the marks.

Another time, we were in grenade training, and I pulled the pin from the grenade and was due to throw it, but my hand froze. The drill sergeant took it from my hand, threw it, threw me to the ground, and called me an F-ing idiot.

On another occasion, volunteers were asked to participate in a police call. I was so excited to be able to join the police and ride around for the day. However, that is not exactly what a police call was. It consisted of picking up trash all over the base. Needless to say, it was not what I expected; however, it did allow me to avoid participating in the obstacle course, which required much dexterity.

After the eight weeks of basic training, I moved to AIT, which is individual training for the specific job for which you are assigned. My specific job was clerical, so I continued on in South Carolina for a four-week period.

In May 1979, I was transferred to my first duty station in Badkreuznach, Germany. I remained there for two years. Germany was a very beautiful place to visit. I loved the cobblestone streets, which were so very clean because the residents swept them on a daily or weekly basis.

Although the country was very beautiful and I thoroughly enjoyed my time there, there was one stain that tarnished the memory of my time there. One night, I was out with my girlfriends at a club, enjoying drinks, laughter, and a good time. As we sat laughing a man approached us and eventually began to pay for our drinks. Throughout the interaction we had with him, he seemed to have an affinity towards me. As the night began to wind down, he invited me to sit in his car with him. I accepted his invitation, while at the same time expressing my desire for him not to move the vehicle.

After sitting in his car for a few minutes, I found my request being denied as he took off in the car and drove directly to the cornfield. On his erratic drive to the cornfield, he began to rip his uniform off. There were buttons flying everywhere. I was very scared of what was going to happen next. Somewhere along the way, he had his hand on my neck, and I thought he was going to choke the life out of me.

Once we reached the cornfield, he stopped the car and he raped me with brute force. After he finished, we remained in the cornfield for a period of time. A few hours later, he told me it is time again. Once again his sexual torture started and eventually ceased. He kept me there for approximately twelve hours before returning me back to the base. Once we reached the base, he said something that surprised and horrified me, at the same time: He said he wanted to marry me. Of course, I denied his request and went inside the base. From there, everything went back to business as usual. I did not report him, and I never mentioned a word of the incident to anyone until sometime much later. Afterwards though, I did notice a change in my behavior. I had already been somewhat promiscuous, but after that incident, my promiscuity increased.

While still stationed in Germany, I met and fell in love with Patrick Brady. He was my first true love, and we engaged in a relationship for year and a half, until he decided to leave the service and move back to Alabama. One tidbit I think would be fair to mention is Patrick was married during the time we had our relationship. However, his marriage did not stop us from sharing an apartment together nor did it stop me from seeking him out once I finished my time at my first duty station and went on to my second duty station in Alabama where he lived.

In 1981, I was sent to Fort McClellan in Annison, Alabama, for one year, for my second duty station. After being there for about six or seven months, I had someone look up Patrick's address, and I went to his home. When I arrived, a woman answered the door, I introduced myself, and we sat on the porch and talked. I told her all about my time with Patrick in Germany, how we were in love, and so on. I went on and on and on, only to discover that I was talking to his wife. Eventually, a cab was called and I was placed in it. Patrick and his wife also got in and the cab driver drove me to an Amway meeting, which is where I was scheduled to be. They dropped me off and rode the cab back home together.

During my second duty, I participated in the military police chemical battalion where we trained with gas masks. During the training, I broke every rule there was to break due to my state of manic depressiveness. I slept with trainees, which was strictly forbidden. I slept with drill sergeants. I took LSD. I had another affair with a married man. I was completely out of control and did not follow rules or regulations. However, throughout all my rule breaking, I managed to do great work.

In 1982, I moved to my third duty station, which was in Indianapolis, Indiana. I trained as a postal clerk for three months. While I was there, I met a woman named Lori Empson who became a good friend of mine. The leader of the platoon had lustful eyes for me and I for him. One evening, we went out to dinner, and later on that night, we engaged in sexual intercourse. The next day, I told Lori how lousy he was in bed, but Lori wasn't convinced of my assessment. so, she decided to have sex with him herself. After she did so, she had to admit that she concurred with my findings.

My last duty station began in 1982 and was in Frankfurt, Germany. I was stationed there for two years and three months. During this last stent of my military career, I had several experiences.

Post Office Girl

I worked at the largest overseas post office while in the army. We handled all the mail for all branches of the military. Every piece of mail every letter every package had to go through Frankfurt. Half of the time I unloaded and loaded 18-wheeler mail trucks. I remember crying when the big catalogs from various department stores would come in. I had to load and unload the heavy catalogs onto the truck by myself and it was a very tiring and daunting task. I also worked in the locator department. When a package was undeliverable, I had to figure out the correct zip code, replace it, and then reroute the package.

Farm Girl

There was a government program or soldiers to pick grapes. I worked in that program for two weeks and I enjoyed it very much. The farmer would put us on a card that was attached to his trailer and drive us to the fields. Each day for the two weeks, we would pick grapes, and we were even permitted to take a bottle of wine home each night.

Winery Debacle

Once when I was walking the streets of Germany, a man drove by and asked if I wanted a ride. I figured he was a safe guy because he had a child in the car with him. Once I got inside the car the man took me to a brewery. While we were inside and walked around the different barrels looking around, and I noticed he kept trying to get next to me. I no longer felt safe, and I grew fearful and began hiding behind the barrels. Finally, I made it to the door and got out of the brewery safely.

Bra Malfunction

Once while running physical training, it was extremely cold outside and when I return to the barracks, I opened my shirt and the T-shirt that I had on underneath had two large blood rings around my breasts. I was horrified and did not understand what had happened to me. I was rushed to the hospital because it was thought I might have cancer. Thankfully, I did not. The tests results were negative. The blood was probably a result of my nipples chaffing from the cold temperatures and rubbing against the interior of my bra as I ran.

The Sick Episode

On a field exercise, I grew very sick with a high temperature and was coughing very hard. I fell on the ground and began hallucinating. I was taking back to the barracks. Because I was on able to participate in my regular duties, my sergeant assigned me to paint the ladies bathroom. Soon, he regretted his decision because I had paint everywhere. For some reason, he did not like me or my shenanigans.

The Christmas Blessing

In the military, there is something known as a Christmas exchange. Certain German families or individuals sponsored Americans who were out of the country without family. I was one of the sponsor raise. A lady sponsored me, and I spent the day with her. She was very kind, fed me soup, and took me into her home for the day. Unfortunately, I do not remember her name; however, I wish I did.

The Love I Lost

While stationed in Frankfurt, I met several soldiers. One was William Davis, call Dada. He was very sweet to me and deeply in love with me. However, I could not reciprocate his love because I had a cage around my heart. He was truly a gentleman and a nice guy. He probably was the best man for me, but I could not accept it at the time. I also had a lover named Terrence Johnson, who was as cold as ice.

He was a military police man and a dog trainer, training dogs to sniff for drugs and explosives. Terrence was also married. Our relationship was purely for sex. When he wanted a booty – he called. He cared for me none. The less he cared, the more I clung. To no avail.

Expect the Unexpected

On one occasion, I found some classified material in a trashcan. I reported the incident to my supervisors because we had Germans working around us on the roofs, etc. and I did not want the material to get into the wrong hands. After reporting the incident, I was treated as though I had done something wrong. I had to talk to a psychiatrist and lay on his couch as if though I were guilty. I was then transferred to another unit. After that, I lost my feelings of loyalty, and I felt betrayed by my superiors.

Mail Deliveries

During my last year of service, I was placed on a mail guard run. On an 18 wheeler, I traveled all throughout Europe delivering mail. I carried my rifle, and people were required to sign for the mail. We carry moneyboxes to other military stations also. That last year was very exciting for me, and there was no more physical training. A bed was set up for me at various stations, and I would get up and deliver mail the next day - riding along with my shotgun and driver. For that job, I was paid extra money – per diem for making the trips.

Throughout my time in the service, I developed friendships with women who were also in the service. Making friends with the ladies was a blast for me. We drank at the NCO clubs and danced. We were confidants. Serving my country allowed me to see much of the world. I travel to Spain, Belgium, Holland, France, and Austria. I completed my military career on August 30, 1984.

A Point to Ponder

Going first to Job Corps and then to serve my country in the U.S. Army was very liberating for me, even with the bumps I experienced along the way. Although there were 'negative' experiences along the way interspersed between the positive experiences, I choose to treasure the sum total of all the experiences because they helped to shape the woman I am today.

~~~~~~~~~~~~~~~

When you find yourself challenged by another person, it is easy to see yourself as a victim and the other person as a bully. However, I would like you to consider this. See the presented challenge as an opportunity to grow to your next level.

If your life is smooth sailing and you never encounter obstacles or challenges, you tend to stay the same. However, challenges come to help us to stretch, develop, mature, and grow to the next level.

Chapter Three ~ Life in the Big Cities

Freedom from the Government

After completing six years of active duty in the United States Army, I was honorably discharged and then proceeded to enlist for four years in the reserves. At that point, I moved to San Diego and lived with my sister Cynthia and her husband Michael for approximately one year. Somewhere along the way, I met a British woman named Rebecca, and after we developed a friendship, I moved into her condominium and lived with her for approximately one year. Throughout that timeframe, Rebecca and I shared some interesting moments, some of which stemmed from our jobs.

Rebecca worked as a waitress and while serving customers, she met a man who took a very strong liking to her. On one occasion, he invited both Rebecca and me over to his apartment. Upon entering, we noticed the coffee table was covered with books on gems and weapons. That gave us an unsettled feeling. To add to the awkward feelings we experienced, his apartment, in general, appeared rather strange to both of us. Simply put, the apartment did not look lived in. Rather, it looked as though it was a place to stop by when he was in town. Despite the lack of warmth in the apartment, the gentleman had a giving heart.

On one occasion, he gave Rebecca pure gems, the value of which were unknown to us. And his extravagant gift giving did not end with Rebecca. On my birthday, he permitted me to drive his Mercedes Benz, and he gave me a pair of $400 diamond earrings and a beautiful silk dress from Macy's. Then suddenly and very unexpectedly, the gift giving ended because he disappeared with no warning and without a trace.

At the same time that Rebecca was involved with the mystery guy, I met and became involved with a man named Michael, and that relationship lasted for about a year. During our time together, in a tumultuous relationship, I met Michael's younger brother, and when

Michael and I would have misunderstandings, his brother was a shoulder to lean on. I would tell him about the things Michael did to me, and contrary to his brother, he was very kind to me. Quite frankly, he treated me better than his brother did, and as a result, I took a liking to him. So, when things fizzled off with Michael, I started a relationship with his brother, which lasted for six months.

But, like anything else that comes to an end, it was time for Rebecca and I to part company. After living with Rebecca for a year, I eventually found an apartment of my own. That was the first time I had ever lived alone, as I had always lived with my siblings and after that I went to the job Corps and then directly into the service. So, I had always been housed with other people. Consequently, I thought the experience of living alone would be nice from not having the nuisance of anyone in my personal space and not having to be in anyone else's.

However, I was in for a rude awakening. My mental illness really kicked in, and I began to have episodes of paranoia. At times, when someone knocked on the door, I would run and hide in a closet. At that time, I could have received medical assistance, but I did not take advantage of the VA benefits I had because frankly I did not understand how their treatment plans and benefits worked. As a result, I suffered in silence.

While still living alone and suffering will my illness, one day I made a trip to the donut shop. There, I ran into a middle-aged black woman who looked destitute. Her outward appearance prompted me to ask her if she had anywhere to go. She responded that she did not, so I invited her to go home with me. She accepted my invitation, and off we went to my apartment. The next day, she asked me to drive her to a bank; I believe it was Bank of America.

At the bank, we both walked in, and I strolled over to the courtesy table where the deposit slips were made available for the bank's clients. Meanwhile, she walked up to one of the tellers and handed them a note that said to give her money and that she was related to former president Ronald Reagan. If I'm not mistaken, she claimed he was her father. The next thing I saw was two bank security officers dragging her out of the bank. I immediately dropped to the floor and rolled under the table, for I did not want anyone to know that the woman was with me. I stayed in my secret position until the men came back inside the bank. At that point, I left.

Three days later, unexpectedly I heard a knock on my door. I opened the door to find the woman standing there. I couldn't believe she had the nerve to return to my home after she had placed me in such a position, so I said to her, "You can't stay here. So, where do you want to go?" She answered, "Santa Barbara." In case you are unaware, that is where Ronald Reagan's ranch is located. So, I drove her to Santa Barbara and dropped her off at the train station. I turned my vehicle around and drove directly back to San Diego.

During that same timeframe, I was working as a sales agent for the Vagabond Hotel. My hours were being tremendously cut, which left me concerned that I would know longer be able to pay my rent. I discussed my situation with my younger sister Catherine, and she suggested I come to Los Angeles and get a job there. I took her advice and moved to Los Angeles with her, where I was able to find a job.

Fancy Free and Footloose

Once in Los Angeles and truly out of the government's hands, as my reserve time had ended, I was fancy free and footloose. I found a job at a telecommunications company, answering inbound calls from different types of companies and taking messages. Due to the sheer volume of calls, I found the job very stressful. However, there were times when there was some excitement because the other operators and I were able to speak with celebrities. I even spoke with a few alleged murderers: Shug Knight, Shante Kimes, and the Menendez brothers. That in itself made the job interesting. I worked quite a bit of overtime, but that did not stop me from being on the prowl for a man and spending the extra cash. My one-stop shop was the $.99 store, and I would buy quite a few trinkets there.

During the course of working that job, I met and began dating Gregory Watts. He turned out to be my worst nightmare. However, I would not find that out until much later. Specifically, when we moved in together and lived in Venice, near the beach. One of the things that proved his nightmarish attitude and behavior was him constantly telling me that he would marry me if I lost weight. His repetitive put down only made me more determined not to adhere to his request.

Another example to demonstrate his mistreatment of me is, one night he and his friend were intoxicated, and he snatched my car keys from me. He and his friend proceeded to take my car for a joyride. In his drunken condition, he drove onto the freeway into oncoming traffic. My Renault was flattened upon impact, and to make matters worse, my insurance had lapsed only nine days prior to the incident. As a result, I was without a vehicle, and I lost my drivers license. Greg and his friend, however, were pried from the car with crowbars and survived the car crash.

As our relationship continued but grew increasingly worse, we eventually broke things off. It took a police escort to assist me in retrieving my belongings from the apartment. Inside, with both my belongings and Greg's, was my sister's radio that I had taken from her home. Because Greg informed the police that the radio was not mine, I was not permitted to remove it from the premises. That enraged me to no end. To enact revenge, I called Goodwill to come and take everything from the apartment, and I also had Southern California Edison to turn off the electricity. When Greg returned home and walked into an empty and dark apartment, he did not know what had hit him. I learned during the course of our relationship that he was a phony Christian, who did not treat me well at all, and on more than one occasion, he threatened to kill me. I was thankful that the relationship was over.

At that point, I went back to my sister Catherine's home for a few days. While I was there, I spoke with my old friend Lori, and she invited me to come to St. Louis. I accepted her invitation, and off I went. I got on the Amtrak train for a three-day journey, which was great fun. I saw one half of the United States on that trip and spent an entire day in Texas, as I made my way to St. Louis.

A Point to Ponder

Life is full of adventure, and everyone should have some sense of adventure in his/her life. My recommendation though is to use caution.

Be careful of your surroundings and be careful of the company you keep. It is great to have the motto of being a Good Samaritan (as illustrated in the Bible), but you must use wisdom and allow the Holy Spirit to lead you with whom you should assist.

Unfortunately, our world is filled with individuals who are looking for people to prey on. Be watchful, so you do not fall prey to anyone.

Chapter Four ~ Meet Me in St. Louis

In January 1992, I arrived in St. Louis with approximately three boxes that held all of the possessions that I had to my name. And to make matters worse, I had no winter coat. Lori met me at the train station and drove me to my new residence. Since that last time I had seen her, she had given birth to a daughter named Autumn, who was a very sweet child, and it was a pleasure to meet her.

After getting myself situated in my new residence, I was able to find a job at Resturia Corporation, which was connected to the Greyhound Bus Station. It was a small fast food place, but the job turned out to be a catastrophe due to my lack of coordination. I was only able to manage working there for three days until things got the best of me. There were many nerve-wracking incidents that occurred in those three days. For example, I would attempt to lift one cup lid, but an extra ten would come along with it and end up spilling all over the floor. It was like a scene from the Lucille Ball Show.

After leaving that job, I took a job at Kirkwood Answering Service as an operator, in the city of Kirkwood, Missouri, which is on the outskirts of St. Louis. I worked there for the entire time I lived in St. Louis, which was approximately three and a half years. I also had a part-time job in downtown St. Louis at a company called Famous Bar. There, I worked as a telephone sales representative, which did not leave me much time to socialize. And without a car, I had to ride the bus to each destination and each job, leaving me even less time.

Amazingly though, I did get involved with a guy. In the course of our brief relationship, I shared how he treated me with Lori, thinking she was my friend and would keep my confidence. But to my surprise, after I broke the relationship off with the guy, she ended up getting together with him.

One day, he accosted me while I was at a bus stop, yelling about something I had shared with Lori in confidence. He nearly knocked me down. At that point, I decided it was best I leave Lori's home and find my own place, after having lived there for a year and a half.

After getting my own apartment, while riding the bus one day, I met another guy whose name was Del Wilson. We developed a friendship, and although he was a married man and had a young daughter, we developed an intimate relationship that lasted for two and a half to three years, while we both lived in St. Louis. At that point, Del moved to Glendale, Arizona, and four months later, I followed his trail. During the four months time while I was still in St. Louis and he was in Arizona, we kept in contact. I made my arrival to Arizona by train, and Del met me and took me to a hotel. We stayed there catching up with one another for the next couple of days. Living in Arizona was quite an adjustment for me because the only person that I knew was Del. Not having a home to go to, I lived at the YWCA for two weeks. After that time, I found a job at an answering service and was able to obtain a studio apartment right next door to the job.

Later, unbeknownst, to me I became involved with a person who was a crackhead. One day, he went to do laundry with all my clothing (bras and panties included) and took off. I had to start a new wardrobe from scratch.

After being on the job for approximately one year, my manager approached me and asked if I was willing to be a nanny for a nine-month-old child and a nine-year-old child. I said yes because I couldn't have my own children, and I desperately had a need to nurture some. Being a nanny was a way to fill the "empty womb" syndrome. But boy, was I in for A surprise. First, the mother, who was known as Big Fat Steph because she weighed over 500 pounds, was very unattractive and mean spirited.

Second, when I entered the home, it was unimaginably filthy. But, I cleaned it inside and out, making it presentable. Third, the nine-year-old child Jeffery had an impacted colon. Steph gave him a particular solution that would assist him in moving his bowels. To ward off accidents, he was required to wear a diaper. His mother would throw the soiled diapers against the shower wall instead of depositing them into the trash receptacle, and I would have to clean up the mess.

Jeffery's father was African, and because Jeffery was biracial, the children at school teased him. Furthermore, he was two grades behind in school. Jordan, the nine-month-old baby, was also biracial, and his father was a drug abuser.

Although I enjoyed the role of nanny, it came with a lot of challenges. Outside of cooking for the children and keeping the home clean, I was also required to go to Jeffery's school in the parental role. Because of Steph's work hours, she was unable to make many of the parent/teacher conferences. To make matters worse, Jeffery was a problem child who liked to light matches on the side of the house and look at magazines that contained erotic images, even at only nine years. Unfortunately, his sexual curiosities did not end with the magazines.

One morning, he put a ladder on the side of the house, climbed up to my bedroom window, and peered through the top of the curtains, in order to have an opportunity to see me naked. When I saw his little face peering over the top of the curtains, I ran outside, grabbed him, and swung him around, while demanding he never do it again. Throughout all of the idiosyncrasies I had to encounter, one perk about my job, in addition to being there to give the children the love they desperately needed, was when Steph bought me a small car to assist me in getting around to do my job more effectively.

Just when I was beginning to manage the house and the children well, my world would be turned upside down. One day to my bewilderment, I came home to find Steph and Del together on my bed. I could not believe my eyes, to say the least. I believe he was with Steph because she had promised to buy him a truck. Their affair added to my diagnosis as manic-depressive was about all I could handle. But, I knew I had to persevere.

A short time later, after plotting a plan, I got a job at an answering service, while still in Steph's employment. One day after work, Del came to pick me up in my car while under the influence of alcohol.

He was very belligerent and tried to choke me. Once we arrived to Steph's house, I took the keys from him and opened the back door. Once inside, I called the police. They arrived and arrested Del. Consequently, he spent one night in jail. He probably would have stayed longer, but Steph ordered me to go with her to get him released.

From that point forward, thoughts of escaping Phoenix was a daily occurrence. However, because I was Jordan's caregiver during the day, I could not leave him alone. So, I had to endure a little while longer.

Eventually, I met a married man named Frank, with home I had a six-month fling. He really knew how to treat a lady. But, I had to bring that relationship to a close because I finally found an opportunity to escape my horrific situation. One day, Jeffery was ill, and he stayed home from school. Both he and Jordan were in their mother's bedroom. While they were preoccupied, I packed all my belongings and slipped out of the house, leaving them to fend for themselves until their mother arrived home later that day. Although Jeffery was only ten years old at the time, I knew he could sufficiently take care of his little brother until their mother arrived.

My leaving was bittersweet. I did not necessarily want to leave the children, but I did need to leave their mother and the horrible situation I have been placed into. Not only that but I had inside information from young Jeffery that his mother had planned to take my car back from me and kick me out of the house. When I heard the words come from his mouth, I was stunned, and said to myself, "Oh no. Who does she think she is?" So when the opportunity presented itself for me to escape, I did just that.

When I made it to the highway, I drove as fast as I could to make my way from Arizona back to California. As soon as I crossed the Arizona/California state line, I stopped and had a steak dinner in celebration of escaping. I could not have been any happier!

A Point to Ponder

At that point in my life, I was offered an opportunity that sounded like a wonderful possibility to earn money and give me a change of pace. However, I did not research the family I would be caring for to find out if there were any red flags. Had I done so, it is possible I could have prevented the entire ordeal. While I loved caring for the children, I could have completely avoided the adult drama.

My advice to anyone who is offered a new opportunity is to do some research to learn as much about the job as possible, especially if the job involves working for a family as in my case.

Everything that sounds good may not be ideal for you!

Chapter Five ~ Back in La-La Land

Once I finished consuming my delicious meal, I drove as fast as I could to Catherine's house to get settled in for the night. I was extremely exhausted from the journey of escaping, so all I wanted to do was lay my head on the pillow. The next day, there was some business I needed to attend to, so off to the DMV I went. When Steph purchased the car, she placed the registration in her name and my name. Specifically, the registration read Steph's name or Cheryl Ryan. Because the word 'and' wasn't there, I was able to remove Steph's name and leave only my name on the registration. I did this to prevent her from coming to retrieve the car or from having to go to court to determine ownership.

A few days later, I called my old job Telecom to see if there were any open positions. To my surprise, there was a position available, so I returned there to work. Upon my return, there were a lot of nice people there and a few crazy ones as well.

Freddy Smith, who changed his name to Freak, was a musician and a good friend of mine. The relationship we had could have possibly become romantic. However, another course of action interrupted the progression of that relationship. I will provide more details on that 'interruption' later.

As the weeks and months passed, I worked a lot of overtime, and my job kept me exhausted. Each day was filled with taking reports. For that, I needed to be on my toes because reports were coming in constantly from Cal OSHA, doctors, lawyers, and even some from construction companies. I would take incoming calls, and I also had to field outgoing calls. That was all the work of a switchboard operator. In the midst of it all, there was at least one perk: I would get some media-worthy news before the media received it. But, on a daily basis, the stress of the workload grew more intense. So for two weeks, I went to group counseling at Kaiser and took some time off work. In the group sessions, the members had different type of stress triggers, not only from work, but also from family, addiction to prescription medicines, alcohol addiction, etc. After spending two weeks in group therapy, I returned to the job.

Reflecting on the time I spent in group therapy, I realized the therapy did not help at all. I discovered I was severely depressed, which caused me to troll the streets looking for love in all the wrong places, as the cliché says. My depression emanated from stress from the job, living the single life, being misunderstood, constantly enduring loneliness, and simply feeling unwanted. As I trolled the streets looking for love, I never found it. I only found weird characters that caused further disruption to my life.

Still working at Telecom, one of my coworkers Carlos and I became good friends. I was still living with Catherine, but Carlos invited me to move into his house and share the rent. I gladly accepted his invitation. Living with Carlos was like attending an endless party. I often referred to his house as the 'den of iniquity,' because he was constantly getting high on marijuana, watching gay porn, as he was a gay individual, and having wild parties. But, at the same time, he made our environment very comfortable with his charming ways and wit. I especially loved when he referred to me by the cute little nickname he had for me, which was Taffy.

Living with Carlos, I learned to expect the unexpected. But I could have never anticipated one particular incident that scared the life out of me. One early morning, when I was on vacation from work, I decided to smoke a joint. As I was enjoying the lift in my spirit from the effects of the marijuana, I began to hear a lot of commotion. Carlos' home phone rang, and the person on the other end asked for him and identified himself as a police officer. Carlos thought it was a friend of his playing a wild and crazy joke. So, he responded, "F*** you!" laughed, and hung up the phone. The officer called back and said, "This is no joke. Look out the window." Before Carlos could respond, officers burst through the door. They swarmed throughout the house like SWAT. They had a warrant for his arrest for a previous occasion where he had thrown rocks at passing cars on the freeway while he was driving. That was an obvious case of road rage. It was my understanding that the victims of the crime had notified the police about the incident, and they had followed up, with the raid being the result. There were twenty officers at the house on that occasion.

Several weeks prior, I began noticing police cars in front of the house or next door. The day before the raid, a helicopter was flying overhead. We were intoxicated and not in our right minds, so we simply waved at them. On the day of the raid, when the officers searched the house, they put handcuffs on me and walked me down a block and a half to put me in a police car, which was parked near the 2 Freeway. I did not have any shoes on, and as a diabetic, that put me in a precarious position. I tried to voice my concern, but they would not adhere to my request of collecting my shoes.

When we reached the police car, they put me in the back of the car and asked me several questions that only pointed to the same thing – whether or not I knew what was going on. I insisted that I did not. One of the officers refuted my response by saying I did know what was going on. I responded once again by telling him that Carlos had not told me anything.

Meanwhile, several other officers, who were outside of the car, kept remarking about how large the house was, as it was over 2000 square feet. The next thing the officers wanted to know was whether or not I had 'anything' on me, and I confessed to having marijuana in my possession. Quickly, they confiscated it. Eventually, after a little more nonsensical bantering, they believed my statement of not knowing anything that was going on as it related to Carlos. They released me, and I had to make the block and a half trek back to the house – barefoot.

Subsequently, Carlos was arrested and held in jail for about a week or so. After he was released, he changed the course of his life, and later, he got a job at a law firm as a paralegal. Although I enjoyed the four-year journey I spent with Carlos, I decided it would be best if I moved out. So, I moved back with Catherine in Lake Balboa, her teenage daughter Brandi, and Brandi's fiancé, Freddie Brown, who was a very good musician but was an ex-con with a drug issue.

To say I was terrified of Freddie was an understatement. To me, his anger turned on and off like a light switch, making him to resemble Dr. Jekyll. He would not let the dog come in at night. I had to hide him. One night, when I was going to the kitchen, I did not expect to see Freddie standing there in partial darkness. His appearance frightened me so much that I jumped extremely hard, and as a result of the jolt, I fell down three flights of stairs. He did nothing to help me.

At that time, we were living in the Los Felix area, on Vermont and Finley. And, my excitement did not end with Freddie. One day after work, I was walking down the street, making my way home. As I looked in the distance, I saw a young man hiding behind a telephone pole while looking at me. I could not understand why he would demonstrate such an absurd behavior. Usually when a man wanted to check out a woman or speak to her, he would simply be direct. But the El Salvadorian, whose name I later learned was Filberto Hernandez, was far from normal.

When I made it to the location where he was standing, he approached me, and we struck up a conversation. He walked with me until I reached the apartment. Upon our arrival, I invited him in. That one invitation led to a year-long love affair, which started on the first night when we made love. I was so in lust with him, completely enamored, that all I saw was his sexiness and nice demeanor. The fact that he was broke did not faze me in the least. Unbeknownst to me, he was living with a French woman and a child. That fact was revealed to me when one day she came to my job. However, my boss at the time, Dennis, did not allow her to speak with me. Instead, he sent her away. After I learned of Filberto's living arrangement and confronted him, the relationship eventually dissipated, as he stopped coming by.

Later, I moved to Sherman Oaks to Tobias Street with Catherine and Benjamin, her boyfriend, who was a member of the group Rolls

Royce before they made it big. At that time, my life was very peaceful, and I continued smoking marijuana to create an environment of tranquility. Furthermore, I kept up my usual activeties of frequenting the $.99 store to buy trinkets and trolling around looking for love, as I once again found myself single.

A year later, I met a guy through the owner of the mechanic shop only to learn that the individual was gay. That was an aspect of his life that he kept from me because he wanted to use me to buy him a cell phone. But the reality of his sexuality was revealed when I saw him at the fair holding hands with a man. When he saw me looking at him, he dropped his hand quickly, but it was too late. The metaphorical cat was out of the bag.

Meanwhile, I was still working at Telcom Communications, like a slave. I continued to suffer serious depression, and I wanted to move back home with my mom and baby sister Angela. However, as fate would have it, an unexpected change occurred. One day, while at work and taking calls as usual, I received a call from Mr. Michael Todd, who was presently the manager for Taurus Construction. That call would prove to change the course of my life.

A Point to Ponder

Be careful of the company you keep! Most people do not wear their non-becoming traits on their sleeves for the world to see. They keep them hidden. And, when you least expect it, they spring them on you.

When developing a relationship with someone you have recently met, take your time with getting to know the person. That way, you are not caught unaware of traits and/or behavior patterns that can be potentially damaging or harmful to you.

Their Story

Michael & Cheryl

Chapter One ~ The Voice

In January 2005, after having rededicated his life to Christ and being single for approximately two and a half years after he having his heart broken, Michael received a call from Robert Hicks, who was starting a new construction company. Hicks invited Michael to be the manager of his company, as Michael had been working construction for ten years at that point. Although Michael had a job for another company, he chose to except the position that Hicks had offered for several reasons: first, the company for which he was presently working did not really care about him as an individual; secondly, Hicks was African-American, and Michael thought it would be honorable to work for someone who was just like him and who was getting his start in the business. Furthermore, Michael had worked with Hicks on other jobs before.

As Michael started on his new journey, each time he will go on break or take lunch, he was required to transfer the calls from the office to his cell phone. To do so, the construction company hired Telcom call center to take their calls while they were out of the office, and if the caller needed to speak with Michael right away, the call was patched into his cell phone. Ironically, each time Michael called Telcom, The same operator would answer his call. What was ironic about that was there were a total of eleven operators who worked for Telcom at that time, but when Michael called, the same operator would receive his call.

As time went on, Michael grew comfortable with the voice on the other end of the phone, which he had learned belonged to Cheryl because she stated her name each and every time she answered incoming calls. She was very polite, and Michael began to feel something each time he heard her voice. The business calls turned to flirting on both sides, each time their lines connected.

At the end of February, Michael asked if he and Cheryl could exchange telephone numbers, so they could call one another while they were away from the office. He made that specific request because their phone relationship had increased as a result of them making small talk each time he called and requested the construction company's calls to be transferred. However, because she was fielding numerous calls continuously, Michael knew they should talk after hours, as not to place her job in jeopardy.

However, once they exchange telephone numbers, it took Michael two weeks to give Cheryl a call. When he did finally call, Sherrill asked him what took so long. He explained to her he had been extremely busy. After the first time they spoke on the telephone in the evening, they would speak nightly for several hours at a time. Then, it seemed as though it would take an inordinate amount of time for them to meet. So, Cheryl told Michael to get on the ball!

A Point to Ponder

Zechariah 4:10 says, *"Do not despise these small beginnings, for the LORD rejoices to see the work begin..."*

Michael was honored to combine his expertise with that of another man to build a company from the ground floor. There was no promise of a great payoff. Nonetheless, Michael went in with his eyes open and dedication in his heart. As a result of his dedication, there was a blessing imbedded within that he could have never foreseen.

Chapter Two ~ Now It's Time to Meet

With Cheryl's prompting, Michael decided to make a move, and they planned to go out on a Sunday because that was the day they were both available, and it just happened to be Mother's Day of 2005. Michael's mother was deceased, and Cheryl's mother lived quite a distance away, so getting together on that day did not prove problematic.

As they waited anxiously for the day they would meet in person, they continued to grow closer through their telephone conversations. They asked each other hard questions, such as would you love me through sickness and in health. And, they both answered yes. Michael also let Cheryl know he was married to God, meaning he was serious about his relationship with God and would not under any circumstances allow anything to interfere with it. Furthermore, he wanted to know if she had an issue with short man. She stated she did not. Meanwhile, Cheryl was still battling depression, and she desperately contemplated going back to live with her mother. But what she was developing with Michael was slowly causing her to change her mind. But she could not be sure. As the day grew closer for them to meet, they began to discuss exactly where they would have their first date.

Cheryl lived in Sherman Oaks, and Michael lived in Los Angeles. They decided to meet in the middle – in Hollywood at Acapulco's. Because Michael had to drive quite a distance to dine with Cheryl, he rented a car because he did not own one of his own. But two weeks later, he purchased a car from his boss for only $300 that he had fixed up for his girlfriend, but she had refused to drive it.

On the evening of the date, Michael showed up three minutes late to the restaurant with a bouquet of beautiful flowers, which was the reason why he was late. When Michael arrived to the lobby of the restaurant, Cheryl rose to her feet when she saw him. He spotted her based on her description of herself, walked up to her, and spoke saying, "Hello, Cheryl," as he handed her the flowers. She thanked him, and at the same time, the hostess approached them and said their table was ready. They promptly followed the waitress to their table. Once they were seated and had placed their order, they began conversing. A while later, their food was delivered to their table, and as they enjoyed a variety of Mexican food, they talked for a period of five hours.

During that five-hour period, Michael called his daughter to share his exciting news about meeting someone whom he was invested in from all the time he had spent with her on the telephone. While speaking to his daughter, Michael placed his hand on Cheryl's knee, thereby claiming her for his own. Both she and he knew what his physical gesture meant. Also while they were dining, Michael sang "Used to be My Girl" by the O'Jays to Cheryl. They were completely enraptured with one another, and nothing else and no one else mattered.

A Point to Ponder

When you know what you want, do not fail to speak up. Go all out! Don't hold back!

Both Michael and Cheryl had a strong desire for one another, and when the opportunity presented itself, they moved forward without hesitation.

Chapter Three ~ Courtship

As Michael and Cheryl continued to date, Michael learned she was an independent woman who had her own car, her own job, and her own place to live. At the same time though, he also learned she needed companionship. So, he set days that he would visit her, which turned out to be Tuesdays and Thursdays. Cheryl informed Michael she had attended culinary school, and when he tasted her cooking he knew she had told him the truth. One week, he was unable to visit Cheryl because he needed to launder his clothing. His plan was to take his clothes to his daughter's home and wash them there. When he told Cheryl about his predicament and being unable to keep their scheduled visit, she told him to bring his clothes to her home and she would wash them for him. Her thoughtfulness was very pleasing to him.

When he arrived to her home, she greeted him at the door along with her dog Kobe, a Welch Corgi. When Michael entered her home and walked past Kobe without acknowledging him, Cheryl quickly 'pulled his coat tail,' correcting him by telling him Kobe was a part of the family. Once Michael understood Kobe's position in the family, he and Cheryl had no problems.

One day, during one of their visits, out of the clear blue sky, Cheryl said, "I have something to tell you." "What?" Michael asked. Cheryl did not answer with words. Instead, she pulled out a large container filled with the files and handed it to Michael. She then looked at him and said, "If you want to leave me, go ahead." The container was filled with files from various doctors, stating Cheryl was manic/depressive. Michael promptly told Cheryl not to worry about her diagnosis. He assured her he was in the relationship for the long haul. From there, they continued to date and go out on dates. One of their dates was to the Comedy Club, and what he considered to be his death trap automobile. (The one he had purchased several months earlier.)

Not much later, Michael had to cancel they are Tuesday and Thursday visits because his vehicle was on its last leg. Cheryl was so disappointment by the reality of their visits being halted that she borrowed $3000 from her boss and took it to Michael. He had no idea she would be stopping by that day, as she wanted to surprise him. After hearing a knock on his door and opening it, Michael was surprised to see Cheryl standing there. When she told him she had stopped by because they were going to buy him a car, he was pleasantly surprised and pleased. He promised he would pay her back, and he did.

During all of their courtship, their feelings grew passionately, and they found themselves constantly in heat for each other. But they stayed in the safe zone by not seeing each other every day.

A Point to Ponder

The courtship is a very important part of a relationship. It is the time during which the two parties take the opportunity to get to know one another: to learn likes, dislikes, temperaments, habits, etc. The longer the courtship, the more the two parties will learn about each other. During this time, it is important to be open and honest, demonstrating one's true self.

Put yourself into the other person's shoes. Would you want to be caught unaware of any personality traits, habits or behaviors? Of course, you wouldn't. Courtships can lead to marriage, and if one is not honest about who he/she is, the other party will get a false idea of the person's true self. Do you want to marry someone you do not truly know? Of course, you don't. Therefore, it is of the utmost importance to reveal your true self, so your partner will know who you are and vice versa. Then, a decision regarding your future can be made.

Chapter Four ~ Engagement & Marriage

One year later, Michael went to his daughter Michelle's house to tell her exactly how he felt about Sharon and that he wanted to marry her. When Michelle heard her father's declaration of love, she told him unequivocally to go ahead and marry Cheryl. Then, she instructed him to purchase to a ring and to not propose without having one. Valuing his daughter's opinion and taking her advice, Michael did as he was instructed. He went shopping and found a ring for Cheryl, and he paid on it little by little until it was paid off.

Once Michael had paid the ring off, he proposed to Cheryl in August, and her bedroom on one knee. Nine months later, they were married on March 2, 2007 and moved to their new home in Long Beach.

Backtracking a few months, Michael's contractor and he went to give a potential client an estimate for her home and the house in the back, which she also own. During the consultation, the client asked if Michael knew anyone who wants to rent the house in the back. He immediately gave Cheryl the woman's telephone number and asked her to give her a call. When Cheryl called the woman, she set up an appointment to have lunch with her to discuss renting the house. After lunch, Cheryl called Michael and told him they were moving into that house in three weeks. Excitedly, Michael said, "we need to get married right away." The next day, they went to the courthouse to get the marriage license. Michael called his pastor and told him that he wanted to get married, and they needed pre-marital counseling. Michael's pastor told him to come right over. Three weeks later, they were married at Faith Central.

After the first couple of years with Cheryl, Michael said to himself, if I knew marriage was this good, I would have done it a long time ago. He learned to have a healthy marriage communication is key. Cheryl and Michael have agreed to disagree. They have excellent communication, and Michael believes couples should grow together, and he and Cheryl have grown together as one. Throughout their time together, Michael has learned to have patience and to treasure his wife; she is his focal point. As the years have progressed, they have grown closer and closer through their family, their love, and their faith. And to add to all of that, one thing that really meant a lot to both of them is that each of their families accepts the other. And, that is just icing on the cake.

A Point to Ponder

When entering into a situation that may be unfamiliar to you, it is always a good idea to obtain advice from someone who is more knowledgeable in the area than you are.

Never be embarrassed about what you don't know. What causes embarrassment is when you had an opportunity to ask and did not.

Chapter Five ~ Draw Closer to God

As an active believer, it was important to Michael to be equally yoked with his wife. Prior to getting married, during their phone relationship, Michael had asked Cheryl about her faith/spirituality. She told him she was raised Catholic, but she was not practicing. Furthermore, she shared with him that she wanted to be a Christian. He was ecstatic about what she had shared with him, and that was one of the reasons he continued to develop a relationship with her. At the time, she was working on Sunday, and even after they were married, she continued to work on Sunday. They began to pray that she would be released from work on Sundays, so she could attend worship services. At that time, Michael was still attending services at Pastor Pittman's church.

One day, God answered their prayers and Cheryl no longer had to work on Sundays. She began attending worship services with her husband and received Christ into her life as her Lord and Savior. After Pastor Pittman's church was dissolved, Pastor Pittman, along with Michael, Cheryl, and several other members shifted their membership to Love, Peace, and Happiness Family Christian Fellowship Church under the leadership of Bishop Leon Martin.

There at LPH, Cheryl started learning the Word by attending worship services and Sunday school. To Michael's delight, she became very inquisitive, and they began to study together. Not much later, after having his heart and spirit touched by Bishop Martin's tutelage, under which he sat, Michael joined the LPH Bible College. Each day after class, he would go home and share all he had learned with his wife. At that point, a deeper desire was sparked within her. She gave him her undivided attention, as he would share the Word of God with her. For that, he loves her so much and gives her the upmost respect.

Each morning, Michael thanks God for his wife, as he reaches over and grabs her hand and they pray together. It did not take him long to realize that the other relationships he had been in had not been blessed by God due to the sin nature within the relationship.

Michael and Cheryl's relationship is growing by leaps and bounds because they continue to keep their eyes on the sparrow.

A Point to Ponder

The Bible tells us to ask for our desires. Michael and Cheryl desired for Cheryl to have Sundays unencumbered with work, so she could attend worship services because her spirit was longing for a relationship with the Lord.

Because of the sincerity embedded in their prayer and the condition of their hearts, God granted their prayer request.

God is no respecter of persons. He will do the same for you!

About the Authors

Michael Todd is a minister of the gospel of Jesus Christ. To prepare for his service as a minister, he attended the LPH Bible Institute while serving as both an usher and deacon.

Cheryl Ryan-Todd is currently retired, after suffering a slight disability.

Both are still active in their church and seek to serve the Lord within their full capabilities.

www.ingramcontent.com/pod-product-compliance
Lightning Source LLC
Chambersburg PA
CBHW060651150426
42813CB00052B/585